MARINE CORPS
SPECIAL OPERATIONS

Simon Rose

AV² provides enriched content that supplements and complements this book. Weigl's AV² books strive to create inspired learning and engage young minds in a total learning experience.

Your AV² Media Enhanced books come alive with...

Audio
Listen to sections of the book read aloud.

Key Words
Study vocabulary, and complete a matching word activity.

Go to www.av2books.com, and enter this book's unique code.

Video
Watch informative video clips.

Quizzes
Test your knowledge.

BOOK CODE

Z 4 5 6 4 3 6

Embedded Weblinks
Gain additional information for research.

Slide Show
View images and captions, and prepare a presentation.

AV² by Weigl brings you media enhanced books that support active learning.

Try This!
Complete activities and hands-on experiments.

... and much, much more!

Published by AV² by Weigl
350 5ᵗʰ Avenue, 59ᵗʰ Floor
New York, NY 10118
Website: www.av2books.com www.weigl.com

Library of Congress Cataloging-in-Publication Data
Rose, Simon.
 Marine Corps Special Operations / Simon Rose.
   p. cm. -- (US Armed Forces)
 Audience: Grade 4-6.
 ISBN 978-1-62127-452-0 (hbk. : alk. paper) -- ISBN 978-1-62127-458-2 (pbk. : alk. paper)
 1. United States. Marine Corps--Juvenile literature. 2. United States. Marine Special Operations Command--Juvenile literature.
3. Special operations (Military science)--Juvenile literature. I. Title.
 VE153.R68 2013
 359.9'6--dc23
                                    2012043464

Printed in the United States of America in North Mankato, Minnesota
1 2 3 4 5 6 7 8 9   17 16 15 14 13

022013
WEP301112

Project Coordinator: Aaron Carr
Designer: Mandy Christiansen

Photo Credits
The photos used in this book are model-released stock images. They are meant to serve as accurate representations of U.S. Special Operations personnel, even though the people in the photos may not be special operators. Weigl acknowledges Getty Images, iStockphoto, Dreamstime, Alamy, and the U.S. Department of Defense as the primary image suppliers for this book.

Every reasonable effort has been made to trace ownership and to obtain permission to reprint copyright material. The publisher would be pleased to have any errors or omissions brought to their attention so that they may be corrected in subsequent printings.

CONTENTS

WHAT ARE MARINE CORPS SPECIAL OPERATIONS?

The United States Marine Corps Special Operations forces are units in the U.S. Marine Corps that take on particularly difficult missions. Special Operations forces carry out most of their operations on land, but they also may use helicopters or other aircraft and ships on missions.

The Marine Corps Special Operations Command (MARSOC) is in charge of all missions related to Marine Corps Special Operations. MARSOC is a division of the United States Special Operations Command (USSOCOM), which includes the special forces of the various branches of the U.S. military. The Department of Defense is in charge of all the branches of the Armed Forces except the Coast Guard. MARSOC has around 2,500 personnel on active duty.

★ Marine Corps Special Operations forces may carry out high-risk combat missions in any kind of terrain.

USSOCOM ORGANIZATIONAL STRUCTURE

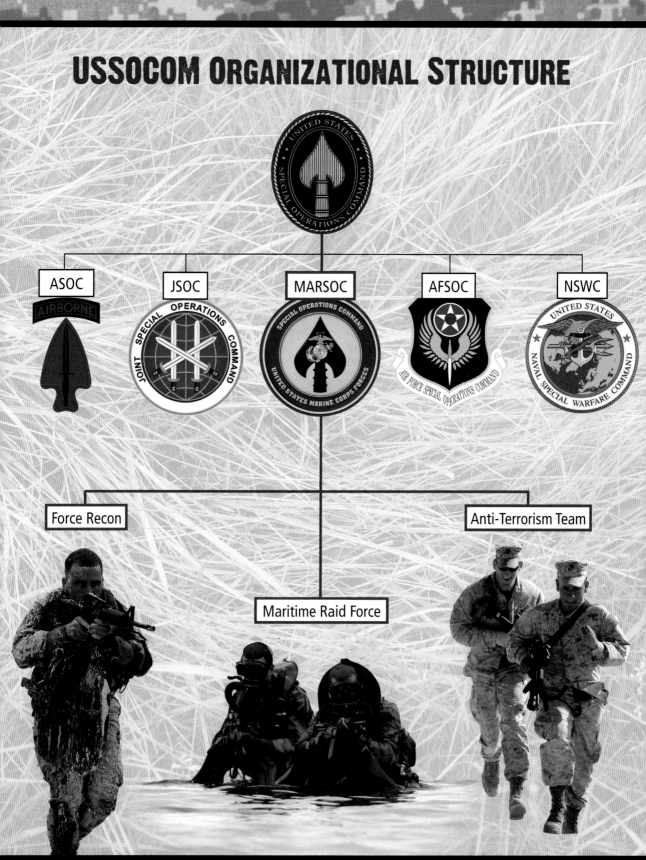

ASOC

JSOC

MARSOC

AFSOC

NSWC

Force Recon

Anti-Terrorism Team

Maritime Raid Force

PROTECTING THE COUNTRY

The Marine Corps Special Operations forces protect the United States and defend its activities and interests around the world. Special operations units perform their duties using rifles, machine guns, and other weapons. In times of war, they work with other special operations groups in the U.S. military and with other branches of the Armed Forces. In peacetime, they stay prepared to take action wherever they are needed.

The Marine Special Operations Regiment is the combat branch of MARSOC. It has three **battalions**, and each battalion has several companies. Every company has special operations teams with a different responsibility. Force Recon is the main **reconnaissance** team, the Maritime Raid Force conducts missions at sea, and the Anti-Terrorism Security Team combats **terrorism**.

On the Front Lines

On the battlefield, Marine Corps Special Operations teams are involved mainly in land-based operations. They often take part in unconventional warfare, such as secret missions behind enemy lines, training soldiers in other countries, and **guerilla warfare**. Marine Corps Special Operations forces carry out missions in many different parts of the world. These missions often prepare the way for larger attacks by the U.S. Armed Forces.

MARSOC FACTS

The Marine Raiders of World War II are thought to have been the first special operations group in the U.S. Armed Forces.

The motto of the United States Marine Corps Special Operations Command is "Always Faithful, Always Forward."

When the United States invaded Iraq in 2003, 1st Force Recon was one of the first U.S. ground troops to enter the country.

MARSOC HISTORY

The Marine Corps Special Operations Command was founded in 2006. However, Marine Corps special operations units have carried out combat missions for many years, including in the wars and battles listed here.

1945
★ World War II ends

1965 TO 1973
★ Force Recon Marines fight in the Vietnam War

1941
★ U.S. enters World War II after the Japanese attack on Pearl Harbor

1945 TO 1949
★ U.S. Marine Corps special units are involved in a civil war in China

1942 TO 1944
★ Marine Raiders conduct operations in the Pacific Ocean

1944

1965

Through the years, Marine Corps special operations forces have taken part in missions throughout the world. They have fought in Asia, Africa, Central America, and the Middle East.

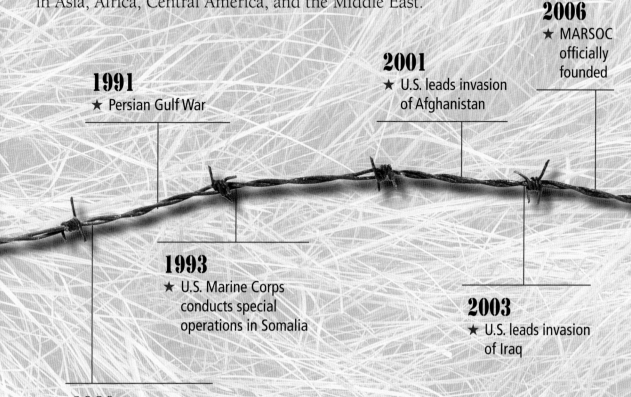

2006
★ MARSOC officially founded

2001
★ U.S. leads invasion of Afghanistan

1991
★ Persian Gulf War

1993
★ U.S. Marine Corps conducts special operations in Somalia

2003
★ U.S. leads invasion of Iraq

1989
★ Marine Corps special units take part in the invasion of Panama

1991

2001

MARSOC AROUND THE WORLD

The Marine Corps Special Operations Command has bases in the United States in North Carolina and California. In most of their missions overseas, Marine Corps Special Operations forces use the same bases as the U.S. Army.

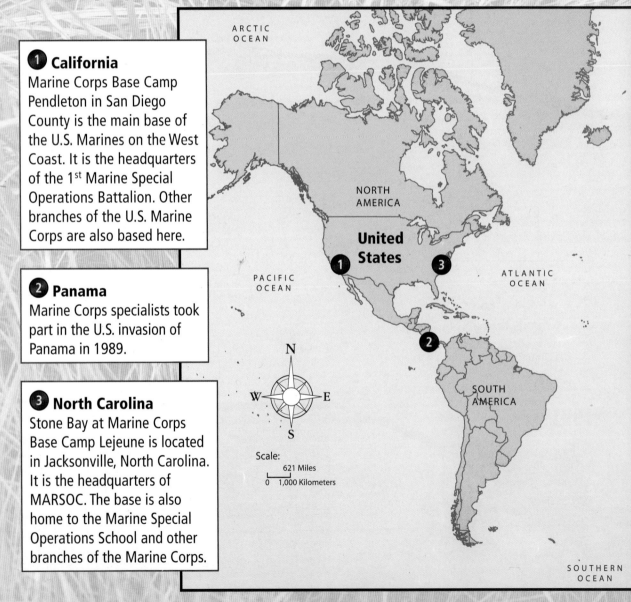

1 California
Marine Corps Base Camp Pendleton in San Diego County is the main base of the U.S. Marines on the West Coast. It is the headquarters of the 1st Marine Special Operations Battalion. Other branches of the U.S. Marine Corps are also based here.

2 Panama
Marine Corps specialists took part in the U.S. invasion of Panama in 1989.

3 North Carolina
Stone Bay at Marine Corps Base Camp Lejeune is located in Jacksonville, North Carolina. It is the headquarters of MARSOC. The base is also home to the Marine Special Operations School and other branches of the Marine Corps.

Scale:
621 Miles
0   1,000 Kilometers

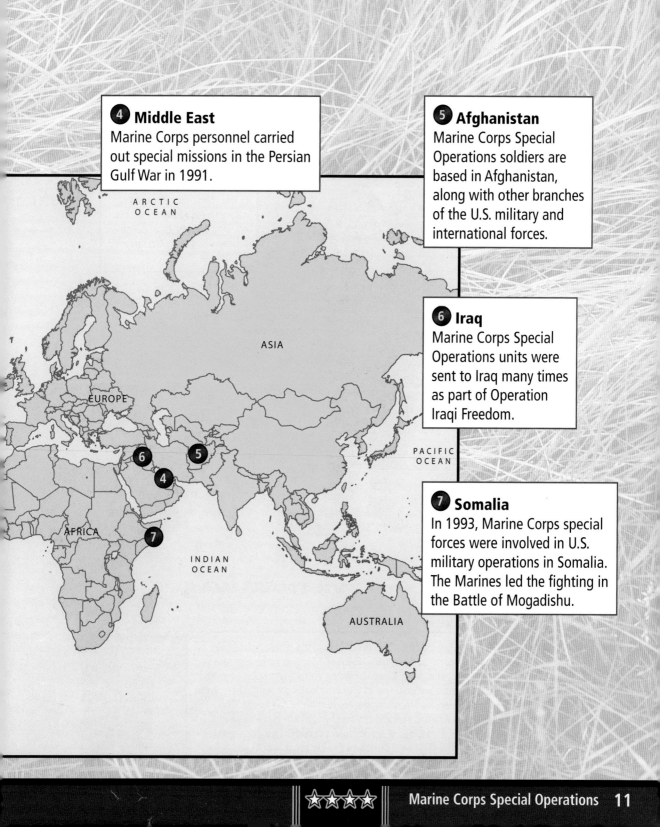

4 Middle East
Marine Corps personnel carried out special missions in the Persian Gulf War in 1991.

5 Afghanistan
Marine Corps Special Operations soldiers are based in Afghanistan, along with other branches of the U.S. military and international forces.

6 Iraq
Marine Corps Special Operations units were sent to Iraq many times as part of Operation Iraqi Freedom.

7 Somalia
In 1993, Marine Corps special forces were involved in U.S. military operations in Somalia. The Marines led the fighting in the Battle of Mogadishu.

ARCTIC OCEAN

ASIA

EUROPE

AFRICA

PACIFIC OCEAN

INDIAN OCEAN

AUSTRALIA

MARSOC UNIFORMS

WORLD WAR II

The M1 helmet was made of steel and weighed 2.2 pounds (1 kilogram). It protected the wearer from **shrapnel** but did not stop bullets. A cloth with a **camouflage** pattern covered the helmet.

The Marine Raiders were specialized Marine units that fought during World War II. Some Marines were issued camouflage uniforms, but most Marine Corps combat uniforms were made of heavy cotton and were dull green. The jacket had a pocket on the chest and two at the hips. It also had three metal buttons down the front.

VIETNAM WAR

U.S. Marines conducted secret operations in the jungle during the Vietnam War. In the early years of the war, Marines wore plain green trousers, shirts, and vests. These uniforms were later replaced with camouflage patterned uniforms of four interlocking colors. There were three versions to blend in with different regions of the jungle. The Lowland version had green and brown shades with black markings. Brown was the main color of the Highland version. The Delta version was similar to the Highland, but it had thicker black markings.

DRESS BLUES

Today, the best-known Marine Corps uniform is the blue dress uniform, often referred to as Dress Blues. This uniform has a long-sleeved, dark blue coat with a high collar. The soldier wears a white, peaked cap with a black visor. **Officers** wear a dark blue belt and other Marines wear a white belt. Medals are worn on the left side of the chest, and ribbons on the right.

Marines wear blue trousers with a red stripe down the outside of each leg.

COMBAT UNIFORM

The Marine combat uniform consists of a long shirt and trousers with a camouflage pattern, a green undershirt, and tan-colored boots. There are different camouflage patterns for different locations and seasons. The desert/summer pattern is tan, brown, and gray, and the woodland/winter pattern is mostly black, brown, and green. Marines also wear a Modular Tactical Vest that protects them from bullets and shrapnel.

MARSOC WEAPONS

WORLD WAR II

M1 Garand Rifle
Marines used the M1 Garand **semiautomatic** rifle during World War II. It could fire 30 rounds of bullets per minute and had a range of up to 500 yards (457 meters). Some Marines were armed with the Thompson **submachine gun**, better known as the Tommy Gun. They also used the bazooka, a gun that fired a small rocket. The gun rested on the shoulder when it was fired. It was used against enemy tanks.

VIETNAM WAR

M16A1 Rifle
The M16A1 was the standard rifle of the U.S. military during the Vietnam War. This lightweight assault rifle could be fired automatically, semiautomatically, or in bursts of three rounds. The **magazine** held either 20 or 30 rounds of ammunition that could be fired in a few seconds in fully automatic mode. The rifle could be fitted with a grenade launcher and other accessories.

TODDY

M4 Rifle
The M4 carbine rifle is one of the main guns used by Marine Corps Special Operations forces. It is a shorter and lighter version of a similar gun, the M16 assault rifle. The M4 operates on gas and can be fired semiautomatically or in three-round bursts. Its barrel is 14.5 inches (37 centimeters) long. The short barrel allows the soldiers to use the rifle in close-range combat.

M107 Rifle
This is a high-powered semiautomatic **sniper** rifle. It can reach targets almost 2,000 yards (1,829 m) away, and the ammunition can tear through body armor and most building materials. The rifle can hit targets behind walls, disable communication equipment or power generators, and rip into armored vehicles.

M32 Multi-Shot Grenade Launcher
The M32 is a hand-held launcher that can shoot six grenades. It can be loaded with any type of grenade used by the U.S. military. All six rounds can be fired in just three seconds. The M32's barrel is 12 inches (30 cm) long and can be fitted with scopes, lighting devices, and other accessories.

JOINING THE MARINES

Anyone wishing to join the U.S. Marine Corps Special Operations must first join the Marine Corps. People must be U.S. citizens or permanent residents, between 17 to 29 years of age, have a high school education, and be in good physical condition. To qualify for officer training programs, people must have a college degree. Some positions in Marine Corps Special Operations units are not open to women.

Applying to the Marine Corps

Step One: Talk to a recruiter

Step Two: Talk to family and friends

Step Three: Submit your application

Step Four: Visit the Military Entrance
Processing Station (MEPS)

OATH OF ENLISTMENT

*❝I do solemnly swear that I will support
and defend the Constitution of the United
States against all enemies, foreign and domestic;
that I will bear true faith and allegiance to the same;
and that I will obey the orders of the President of the
United States and the orders of the officers appointed
over me, according to regulations and the Uniform
Code of Military Justice. So help me God.❞*

Boot Camp Basic training for the Marine Corps
is often called Boot Camp. Recruits who apply
for the special forces must go through a selection
process. Next comes the Individual Training
Course (ITC), one of the toughest training
programs in the U.S. military. The ITC lasts for
seven months and includes training in physical
fitness, hand-to-hand combat, swimming,
survival techniques, and weapons.

All special operations Marines have training in
foreign languages, and some may attend the
Advanced Linguistics Course. Once they are
assigned to their battalion, training continues
for 18 months. Special operations soldiers also
take the Marines Combatant Diver Course and
attend the Army's Airborne School. Courses are
also offered in specialized areas, such as advanced
reconnaissance or sniper training.

JOBS IN THE MARINES

Being a member of a Marine Corps Special Operations team is not just about serving in combat. There are many types of careers for special operations personnel. There are jobs in **military intelligence**, communications, electronics, and health and medicine. There are jobs working with computers and technology, and jobs for language experts. The training and experience gained in the Marines can also lead to successful careers in **civilian** life after military service is completed.

Communications and Technology

These types of jobs involve working with computers and other types of electronic equipment. There are jobs in computer programming, communications systems, and different types of technical support.

Linguists and Interpreters

Marine Corps Special Operations personnel spend much of their military career on missions in foreign countries. There are careers for those with detailed knowledge of different cultures and for **linguists** who can read, write, and speak foreign languages. Jobs involve translating and interpreting languages to help military personnel operate more effectively.

Health Care and Medicine

Careers in health care and medicine include working as doctors, nurses, and dentists. Other jobs involve managing health care facilities, laboratory research, and operating medical tools such as X-ray and ultrasound equipment.

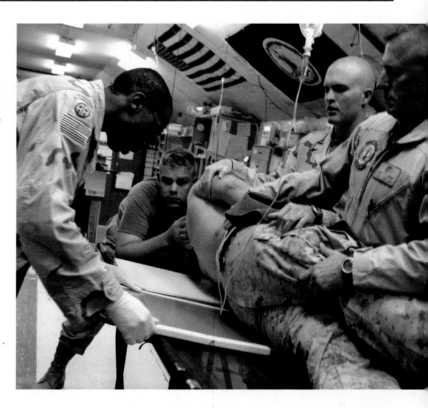

COMMUNITY LIFE

Life for Marine Corps Special Operations personnel is much like civilian life. Personnel work regular hours at a job, they spend time with their families, and they fill their free time with hobbies, sports, and other activities. Some personnel live in barracks, but others live in houses either on or off the base.

Many bases where Marine Corps Special Operations soldiers are stationed have all the facilities of most towns and cities. This may include hospitals, schools, day care centers, libraries, sports facilities, and shopping malls. MARSOC provides a wide variety of programs to improve the quality of life for families living on military bases. These include counseling services, programs to improve on-base education and job opportunities for family members, and programs that help families deal with the stress of having a parent working in a combat area overseas.

★ Many Marine Corps Special Operations personnel are married and have children.

WRITE YOUR STORY

If you apply to join the Marine Corps, you will probably need to write an essay about yourself. This is also true when you apply to a college or for a job. Practice telling your story by completing this writing activity.

1
Brainstorming
Start by making notes about your interests. What are your hobbies? Do you like to read? Are you more interested in computers or power tools? Then, organize your ideas into an outline, with a clear beginning, middle, and end.

2
Writing the First Draft
A first draft does not have to be perfect. Try to get the story written. Then, read it to see if it makes sense. It will probably need revision. Even the most famous writers edit their work many times before it is completed.

3
Editing
Go through your story and remove anything that is repeated or not needed. Also, add any missing information that should be included. Be sure the text makes sense and is easy to read.

4
Proofreading
The proofreading is where you check spelling, grammar, and punctuation. You will often find mistakes that you missed during the editing stage. Always look for ways to make your writing the best it can be.

5
Submitting Your Story
When your text is finished, it is time to submit your story, along with any other application materials. A good essay will increase your chances of being accepted, whether it be for a school, a job, or the Marines.

TEST YOUR KNOWLEDGE

1 What does MARSOC stand for?

2 How many personnel serve in MARSOC?

3 When was MARSOC founded?

4 Where is the MARSOC headquarters located?

5 What is the best-known Marine Corps uniform?

6 What was the main rifle used by the U.S. military in the Vietnam War?

7 What is the motto of MARSOC?

8 What was the name of specialized Marine units in World War II?

9 How many rounds can the M32 Grenade Launcher fire?

10 How long does the Individual Training Course (ITC) last?

Answers: 1. Marine Corps Special Operations Command 2. About 2,500 3. 2006 4. Stone Bay at Marine Corps Base Camp Lejeune in North Carolina 5. Dress Blues 6. The M16A1 7. "Always Faithful, Always Forward" 8. The Marine Raiders 9. Six 10. Seven months

KEY WORDS

battalion: a military unit with 300 to 1,200 soldiers; several battalions usually form a regiment or a brigade

camouflage: clothing or other items designed to blend in with the surroundings

civilian: a person who is not a member of the military

guerilla warfare: unexpected attacks by small groups of troops within areas occupied by the enemy

linguists: people who specialize in reading, writing, and translating foreign languages

magazine: the part of a firearm in which ammunition is stored and fed into the weapon

military intelligence: information about the armed forces of another country

officers: soldiers who are in positions of authority

reconnaissance: exploration of an area to gather useful information

semiautomatic: a gun that can fire a round of bullets and load a new round each time the trigger is pulled

shrapnel: pieces of metal that fly out of a bullet or bomb when it explodes

sniper: a highly trained marksman who shoots at enemies from concealed locations or long distances without being detected

submachine gun: a lightweight automatic gun that shoots pistol-type bullets

terrorism: the use of violence or threats to harm or create fear within a country

INDEX

Log on to www.av2books.com

AV[2] by Weigl brings you media enhanced books that support active learning. Go to www.av2books.com, and enter the special code found on page 2 of this book. You will gain access to enriched and enhanced content that supplements and complements this book. Content includes video, audio, weblinks, quizzes, a slide show, and activities.

AV[2] Online Navigation

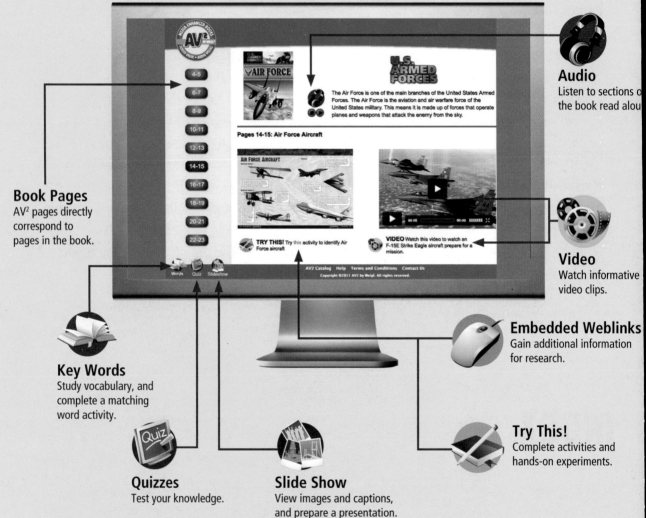

Book Pages
AV[2] pages directly correspond to pages in the book.

Audio
Listen to sections o the book read alou

Video
Watch informative video clips.

Embedded Weblinks
Gain additional information for research.

Key Words
Study vocabulary, and complete a matching word activity.

Quizzes
Test your knowledge.

Slide Show
View images and captions, and prepare a presentation.

Try This!
Complete activities and hands-on experiments.

AV[2] was built to bridge the gap between print and digital. We encourage you to tell us what you like and what you want to see in the future.

Sign up to be an AV[2] Ambassador at www.av2books.com/ambassador.

Due to the dynamic nature of the Internet, some of the URLs and activities provided as part of AV[2] by Weigl may have changed or ceased to exist. AV[2] by Weigl accepts no responsibility for any such changes. All media enhanced books are regularly monitored to update addresses and sites in a timely manner. Contact AV[2] by Weigl at 1-866-649-3445 or av2books@weigl.com with any questions, comments, or feedback.